Read & Resp

Ages 7–11

Read & Respond

Ages 7–11

Author: Eileen Jones

Commissioning Editor: Rachel Mackinnon

Editor: Roanne Charles

Assistant Editor: Kim Vernon

Series Designer: Anna Oliwa

Designer: Dan Prescott

Text © 2011 Eileen Jones © 2011 Scholastic Ltd

Designed using Adobe InDesign

Published by Scholastic Ltd,
Book End, Range Road, Witney,
Oxfordshire OX29 0YD
www.scholastic.co.uk

Printed by Bell & Bain

7 8 9   6 7 8 9 0

British Library Cataloguing-in-Publication Data
A catalogue record for this book is available from the British Library.

ISBN 978-1407-12704-0

Acknowledgements

The publishers gratefully acknowledge permission to reproduce the following copyright material: **Walker Books** for the use of the cover, text and illustrations from *Greek Myths* retold by Marcia Williams. Text and illustrations © 1991, 2006 Marcia Williams (1991, Walker Books). Every effort has been made to trace copyright holders for the works reproduced in this book, and the publishers apologise for any inadvertent omissions.

Greek Myths

About the book

Greek Myths is another wonderful book in which Marcia Williams uses her distinctive comic-strip style to retell tales. Funny yet serious, the book provides simple knowledge of Greek mythology and is ideal for Key Stage 2 study. Entertaining, exciting and accessible, the book ties in to many Literacy Framework genres: its style is cartoon; its basis is myths; these contain mystery and adventure; they are from another culture; and they raise issues and dilemmas.

The myths are set in ancient Greece and its islands, where people believed that they lived under the gaze of their gods on Mount Olympus. So, characters' exploits are often performed to please or appease the gods.

The first myth in the book describes the creation of mankind. The giant Prometheus creates people, but they are given life by Zeus, king of the gods. People must remember their place and respect the gods. It is in an act of vain disobedience, when Pandora opens the special box, that mankind's sufferings begin. Pandora releases evils, including some that are explored in other myths: greed that banishes Arion's sailors to *an ugly, barbarous land*; mistrust that separates Orpheus and Eurydice; and pride that condemns Arachne to a life of weaving; jealousy that results in the death of Daedalus' son;

Gods and people always demand revenge. Theseus cannot ignore King Minos' cruelty, so he kills the Minotaur, only to endure his father's suicide. Are the gods exacting revenge for his desertion of Ariadne? Implication adds mystery.

The myths are told through three vehicles: detailed illustrations, serious captions, and humorous speech bubbles. The witty comic strips are there to be pored over, and each reading reveals new visual humour and jokes initially overlooked. It is a book that continues to be irresistibly entertaining.

About the author

Marcia Williams is the daughter of a writer (her mother) and a playwright and theatre director (her father). She spent her early childhood in Canton (China), Hong Kong, Nigeria and the Middle East. She loved books from an early age and was fascinated by the illustrations. She remembers that fairy tales often frightened her, but she never wanted them to end. While her parents travelled overseas, she attended a boarding school in Sussex. Her weekly letters to her parents were full of illustrations.

As an adult, she had a number of jobs, but it was as a nursery teacher that she discovered her talent for storytelling. She wrote and illustrated *The First Christmas* in 1987.

Marcia Williams lives in London. She has two grown-up children, three grandchildren, a cat, and a dog 'bigger than a Shetland pony'.

Facts and figures

Greek Myths

Published: 1991, Walker Books.

Most of Marcia Williams' books are in cartoon-strip style and many are retellings of famous tales from the past. They include *King Arthur and the Knights of the Round Table* and *The Adventures of Robin Hood*. Two of her books make Shakespeare's plays accessible to children: *Bravo, Mr William Shakespeare!* and *Mr William Shakespeare's Plays*.

Guided reading

Introducing the book

Begin with the front cover. Comment on the position and typography of the title, designed to attract and inform quickly. Check the children's understanding of 'myths'. Agree that they are stories from ancient times about gods and goddesses, heroic characters, strange creatures and supernatural phenomena.

Ask: *Who is this book's author? Who is the illustrator?* (Marcia Williams is both.) Point out the word *retold*, revealing that these are rewritten versions of established stories. Seek responses to the cover. *Is it attractive?* Comment that the illustration style makes the book appear less serious and 'dry' than the title might suggest.

Look for information on the back cover. Is it helpful? Does it encourage the children to read the book? (We see which myths are included, favourable reviews from famous people and publications, and more amusing and intriguing illustrations.)

Pandora's Box

Read most of the first page (up to *harmony reigned...*), initially reading the text captions before exploring the pictures and speech bubbles. Ask: *What format is this?* (Cartoon strip.) Contrast the main text's plain formality with the pictures' humour and modern, conversational language. Do the styles balance? Identify the setting of place and time (*In the beginning*) and the introduction of characters: Zeus and the gods on Olympus; Prometheus and mankind on earth. Discuss this opening's function: to hook the reader for this myth and the book. Are the children hooked?

Read about Prometheus' misdemeanours and Pandora's disobedience. Establish themes: respect for authority, arrogance, revenge. Identify Prometheus' punishments: fire is extinguished, then he is chained to a rock and attacked by a vulture. Who suffers because of Pandora's treachery? (Mankind.) Pick out the strong words on the final page (*evil, spite, pain,*

sorrow, infesting, despair) and the picture's vivid anger and movement. Ask: *What escapes from the box?* (Everything that harms mankind.) *Why is hope important?* (It saves people from total unhappiness.)

Arion and the Dolphins

Read as far as Arion's departure. Comment on the dancing liveliness of the first two pictures. Discuss the marrying of pictures and text in *So when Arion...* and *Finally...* (rows of small figures pacing back and forth suggest considerable thinking time). Ask: *In the final picture, why does the repeated ship's colour fade?* (Arion's ship is moving further away as darkness comes.)

On the second page, explore character development: Arion is loyal (keeping his word to Periander, he is returning); quick-thinking (when singing, he asks the gods' protection); resourceful (he takes his lyre into the sea). Compare this with the crew's disloyalty, greed and violence.

Read the final pages. Ask: *Does Arion's musical instrument prove important?* (It helps him to sing and so attract the dolphins.) Comment on *I'll get my revenge!* – a common theme in myths. In contrast, how does Arion show further goodness? (He is *more merciful*.) Examine the details of the final cartoon and how well it illustrates the text.

Orpheus and Eurydice

Read the first two pages. Ask: *What is different about this myth's presentation?* (There are no speech bubbles.) Comment on the light colours and happy movement at the beginning. Investigate changes during Orpheus' journey to the River Styx and establish how the length of the journey is emphasised: through sequential detail in long, narrow picture strips. Examine the details, such as making a fire, climbing a tree, sheltering from rain, struggling to walk. Ask: *Why does Charon look so strange?* Suggest that he is half living and half dead. Identify the lyre's importance now: it helps to persuade Charon. Refer to music's similar power in 'Arion and the Dolphins'.

Read the last two pages. Explore the depiction of the *dark and grey* asphodel fields and explain that dead people, after a mixture of good and bad lives, live in these fields; they eat asphodel flowers. Look at the fantastical Cerberus with his three dog heads and two snake heads. Ask: *What proves that Orpheus is a powerful storyteller?* (Pluto and Persephone weep and grant his request.) *What is their condition?* (Orpheus must not look back to check that Eurydice is following.) Examine the detail of the cartoon strips depicting Orpheus's return journey. Ask: *What are the ghosts doing?* (Teasing and tempting.) *Orpheus manages not to turn around until when?* (At the boat.)

The Twelve Tasks of Heracles

Read the first page. Identify important facts about Heracles: he has great strength; Hera is an enemy; he wants the gods' forgiveness for the deaths of his children. Explain the fifth cartoon: *Hercules* is the equivalent Roman name. Can the children tell you which word makes the tasks sound impossible? (*Deadly.*)

Study the first four tasks. Ask: *What is significant about the animals' supernatural capabilities?* (Success over them emphasises Heracles' strength.) Enjoy the humour, noting the King's repeated hiding.

Investigate the crowded strips of the next five tasks. Ask: *What impression is given?* (The tasks need work and time.) Why does Heracles say, *'I'm not just a muscle man'?* (He also uses intelligence.) Track the ongoing joke of the King's cowardice. Invite the children to read out the cartoon dialogue in the eighth task. Had they noticed Hera?

Read the last page. How is extended time confirmed? (Heracles has been working for *ten years*.) Explore his use of cunning with Atlas and persuasion with Cerberus. Which word confirms he is forgiven? (*Pardoned*.) What is his extra 'prize'? (Hera gives up.) Find the King in the border. Ask: *Is this the funniest myth so far?*

Daedalus and Icarus

Read the first page. Check the children's understanding of the early part. *What happens when Talos falls?* (Athene turns his spirit into a partridge.) *Why does Daedalus flee?* (He fears punishment for killing him.) *Why does he build the Labyrinth?* (To contain the King's man-eating Minotaur.)

Read the next page. What do the children think makes Icarus forget his father's warning? (He is *overwhelmed with the joy of flying*.) Invite the children to answer the proverb question in the bird's speech bubble: 'Pride comes before a fall'. Explain that 'fall' is usually used figuratively for a mistake; here it is a literal drop from the sky.

Look at the full-page illustration on the third page and note how Icarus is *surrounded*.

Comment on the sky's later change of colour. Icarus moves from the sun's light, but could darkness also represent impending disaster? Ask: *Does Daedalus think his son's death was an accident?* (He believes that the gods were involved.)

Perseus and the Gorgon's Head

Read the first two pages up to ...*snake-covered head*. Explain *oracle* in the second picture: a holy person foretelling the future. Ask: *What has Acrisius been told?* (His grandson will kill him.) Comment on the small pictures emphasising the eventful journey to Seriphos.

Discuss why Perseus' mission is *deadly*. (Just a look from the snake-haired Medusa or her sisters would turn people to stone.) Read the rest of the story. Compare the use of the repeated figure ascending Mount Atlas with the ship in 'Arion and the Dolphins'.

Explore the Grey Ones' humorous squabbles and how Perseus gets information. Ask the children why he calls out *'HERMES BEWARE!'*? (He can fly too now.) Point out his watchful flight and speedy dispatch of Medusa. Ask: *Why does Perseus put on the helmet?* (To escape the sisters.) Examine the homeward journey's dangers and

Guided reading

battles, and identify the time reference: *after a year away*.

Comment on Perseus' clever treatment of Polydectes: Medusa's head is pulled out at him. Enjoy the animals' witty dialogue and revise Dictys' identity from early in the myth. Note the final text which shows that the oracle's prediction will come true.

Theseus and the Minotaur

Read through the first two pages. Revise references to Minos, the Labyrinth and Minotaur in 'Daedalus and Icarus'. Recall that sacrifice is usually to gods. Ask: *Who is this sacrifice to?* (The Minotaur, for Minos, to avoid war.) Discuss Theseus' heroism and his dog's mournful farewell.

Examine the illustration of the voyage. Then read on and ask: *In Crete, who falls in love with whom?* (Ariadne loves Theseus. His feelings are unmentioned.)

Identify evidence of death in the Labyrinth on the third page. Ask: *How do bats, rats and spiders support the text?* (They prefer *cold, dark* places.) *Why is* ROAR! *in large upper case?* (To show the surprise and volume.)

Ask the children why the first strip on the last page has five similar pictures ending in graphic detail. (To portray the *long and fierce* struggle.) Why does Theseus bring out the Minotaur's head? (As proof of its defeat.) Consider how the thread is *magic*. (Perhaps it cannot break.)

Speculate on why Theseus abandons Ariadne. Note the dog's reappearance, then study the final text. Ask: *Is it a totally happy ending? Is Theseus punished for abandoning Ariadne as well as being forgetful?* (*Thoughtless* is ambiguous.)

Arachne versus Athene

Read the first two pages. Comment that our very first impression of Arachne is an unpleasant one, through her speech bubble and ...*not a very beautiful girl, or a very nice one.* Ask: *What is emphasised by six pictures within one frame?* (Frequency and repetition.) Pick out the adjective *arrogant*. Do the children think it explains Arachne's claim to be *even cleverer than* Athene?

Notice Athene's owl, representing wisdom, and consider her fairness: in disguise, she tries to reason with Arachne. Ask: *Which adjective suggests future victory?* (*All-powerful.*) Why is Arachne unafraid? (She is *foolish*.)

Read the rest of the story. Contrast the finished cloths: Athene's presents the gods as glorious; Arachne's insults them. *How is Athene's fury expressed?*

Explore the humour of the two small pictures: Arachne's father struggles to think of a redeeming quality to save her. What do the children think *grudgingly* warns? (Athene will still punish Arachne.) Identify confirmation of this in *dreadful* and Athene's smile. Consider how *fine, silken thread* hints at Arachne's former weaving brilliance.

Shared reading

Extract 1

● This first page of 'Arion and the Dolphins' succinctly introduces characters, setting and plot. The book's second myth, it further familiarises the reader with the author-illustrator's style.

● Focus on the opening caption. What information is given? (Setting and characters.) What is the tone? (Serious.)

● Highlight *music lover* and note its formality. Then look at Periander's speech bubble, inviting half the class to read it out. How does it sound? (Casual, modern, funny.)

● Run the same comparison with *favourite star*

and its accompanying 'HELLO FANS!' speech bubble.

● What is distinctive about the fourth cartoon? (Rows and direction-changes emphasise time and pace.) Identify this device in the sixth cartoon showing repeated pleas and refusals. Ask: *What eventually persuades Periander?* (Prize money.) Look at the last Arion figure. *What emotion is shown?* (Shock.)

● Remark on the final caption's brevity, and circle *ship*. Contrast the large cartoon's detail and use of *four* ships to show the ship moving away.

Extract 2

● In this final part of 'Daedalus and Icarus', the sun's heat affects Icarus.

● Circle *suddenly, felt, melt, floating*. Mark the interpretation of the words in the first picture: the baffled face and movement of wax and feathers.

● Point out the fallen arms in the gloomy second cartoon, matching *would not hold up*. Circle *plunged*. What does this encapsulate? (Speed and force.)

● Why is the third frame divided? (To show the extended, frantic search.) Read the next cartoon's caption and look at the mournful face. With Track Icarus' gaze to the *few feathers*.

● Circle and define *hovered*. Then compare it with the stiff body that *floated*. Continue to emphasise the interdependence of captions and cartoons when there are few speech bubbles. Circle the understated *weeping* and *gently* and mark the translation into powerful facial expression and body language.

● Identify the partridge (Talos). In the final text, circle *knew* and *at last*. Do the children think Daedalus has been expecting punishment? Point out Daedalus' gentle stroking. Is he sorry for what he did to Talos? Is he treating the partridge as a substitute son?

Extract 3

● This is the final part of 'Arachne versus Athene', when Arachne is hanging from a beam.

● Point out the first frame's dividing line and ask: *Why is it used?* (To mark Athene's long wait for a *good reason*.) Read the first caption and circle *grudgingly*. Does this hint at at least *some* future punishment? Which later words confirm terrible change? (*Dreadful transformation*.)

● Create three oral reading groups (captions, Athene, Arachne) for the first strip. After the performance, ask: *Do the speech bubbles lighten the tone?*

● Examine Arachne's eyes in the second strip. Ask: *What emotions are shown?* (Arachne's

eyes show bewilderment and anger, horror, frustration.)

● Circle *cleaved*, and draw lines to the fingers. Ask: *What has happened? What does 'cleaved' mean?* (Stuck.)

● Circle *shrank*. Draw a measurement line to indicate the position of Arachne and her speech bubble further back in the sixth frame. Discuss the effect.

● Underline the penultimate caption. Will the *fine, silken thread* make Arachne happy or frustrated? Then circle *revenge*. Why is this appropriate in this, the book's final text? (Revenge is the outcome of many myths.)

Extract 1

Arion and the Dolphins

Like most Greeks, Periander, King of Corinth, was a music lover.

His court was crowded with singers and musicians.

But his favourite star was Arion. Arion's music always put Periander in a good mood.

So when Arion asked to visit Sicily for a music festival, Periander hated the idea.

"I shall be out of humour all the time you're away," he declared gloomily.

Finally Arion convinced him that it would be worth all the prize money he would win.

So a ship was rigged and manned and Arion set sail for Sicily.

Shared reading

Extract 2

Daedalus and Icarus

Daedalus believed it to be the spirit of his nephew, Talos, and he knew that the gods had at last punished him, by allowing Icarus to fall to his death – just as Talos had done.

Text and illustrations © 1991, 2006 Marcia Williams.

Extract 3

Arachne versus Athene

Grudgingly, the goddess agreed to let her rival live.

She sprinkled herbs upon Arachne – and there began a dreadful transformation.

First, Arachne's hair fell out.

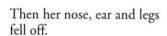

Then her nose, ear and legs fell off.

Her arms disappeared, so that her fingers cleaved to her sides.

Her head and body shrank, until she was no bigger than a fist.

And finally, the rope by which Arachne dangled became a fine, silken thread.

Athene had taken her revenge – she had turned the boastful Arachne into a spider!

Text and illustrations © 1991, 2006 Marcia Williams.

Plot, character and setting

Understanding character

> **Objective:** To deduce characters' reasons for their behaviour from their actions.
> **What you need:** Copies of *Greek Myths*, photocopiable page 15, writing materials.
> **Cross-curricular link:** PSHE.

What to do

● Read 'Pandora's Box'.
● Guide the children in scanning the text and revising events. Suggest that there are four main characters and ask the children to identify them. (Zeus, Prometheus, Pandora, Epimetheus.) Ask: *Who is the most important person for this myth?* Suggest Pandora because of the title and what she does, even though we do not meet her until halfway through.
● Share ideas on how Marcia Williams reveals characters' personalities. Captions give some information, but most information is in the pictures and speech bubbles. For example, when Zeus receives guts and eyeballs, the picture and speech tell the reader of his quick temper. Suggest that the text offers traditional characterisation of these 'historical' figures; in the cartoons, Williams adds her modern interpretation.
● Direct the children to the third page, and hand out photocopiable page 15. Advise the children to concentrate on one cartoon at a time and work with a partner, checking where each incident occurs and the context for Pandora's behaviour. From the evidence of each cartoon, which adjectives best describe her?
● Ask the children to write four new adjectives, one for each cartoon.

> **Differentiation**
> **For older/more confident learners:** Ask the children to add the cartoon where Pandora has captured the box and write three adjectives to suit her then. Progress to a full character sketch of Pandora.
> **For younger/less confident learners:** Reduce the choice of adjectives, leaving only the most appropriate.

Collecting information

> **Objective:** To identify and summarise evidence from a text to support a hypothesis.
> **What you need:** Copies of *Greek Myths*, photocopiable page 16, writing materials.
> **Cross-curricular link:** Geography.

What to do

● Read to the end of the second page of 'Arion and the Dolphins'. When posing the questions suggested here, encourage partner discussion before progressing to whole-class exchanges.
● Guide the children in scanning the first two pages. Ask: *Where is the story set?* (Corinth, Sicily and the sea between.) *Which characters are important?* (Periander, Arion and the sailors.) *What do we learn about them?*
● Give out photocopiable page 16. Ask the children to fill in the 'What I know…' section, summarising their information so far.
● Identify some unanswered questions: Will Arion be saved? Will Periander see him again? Where will the sailors go? Ask the children to summarise missing information in 'What I don't yet know…'.
● Point out Dolphins in the title and note that they have not appeared in the story yet. Recall the similar 'Pandora's Box', and make the point that its themes of punishment and revenge are common to myths.
● Invite the children to write a prediction for this plot. Advise them to consider the title, what they know already and their knowledge of other myths. Encourage them to listen to one another's ideas, and then see whether they are correct.

> **Differentiation**
> **For older/more confident learners:** Widen the study of known and unknown to include the music prizes.
> **For younger/less confident learners:** Make partner discussion a preparation for mainly pictorial recording of answers.

Plot, character and setting

Words and pictures

> **Objective:** To use layout and format for different purposes.
> **What you need:** Copies of *Greek Myths*, writing materials.
> **Cross-curricular link:** Design and technology.

What to do
- Read 'Orpheus and Eurydice'.
- Discuss Marcia Williams' dual role as author and illustrator, producing a strong partnership between words and pictures.
- Give out individual sheets of paper for the children to: turn sideways (landscape); divide into two columns ('Words' and 'Pictures'); and fold into four rows/strips.
- Direct them to the myth's first caption. Which adjectives, verbs and phrase are important? Agree on *famous, came, play, sing* and *all over Greece*. Ask the children to write these under the first row's 'Words' heading.
- Explore how these words are illustrated in the first picture strip: Orpheus' size and prominence; numerous listeners; people travelling towards him. Ask the children to write their comments under the first row's 'Pictures' heading.
- Repeat this for the second strip, using partner before class discussion. Identify effective adjectives, *wild, tame, beautiful* and *happiest*; the powerful verb, *bend*; ordinary verbs, *made, loved* and *married*. Explore the pictorial representation: smiling, leaning trees; docile animals; flowers and happy faces in the wedding procession. Let the children write their thoughts for the second strip.
- Invite partners to investigate captions and pictures for the last two strips of the page, and to summarise their ideas on their sheets.

> **Differentiation**
> **For older/more confident learners:** Include page two of 'Orpheus and Eurydice'.
> **For younger/less confident learners:** Offer suggestions and accept less writing.

Serious or funny?

> **Objective:** To identify features that writers use to provoke readers' reactions.
> **What you need:** Copies of *Greek Myths*, writing materials.
> **Cross-curricular link:** Art and design.

What to do
- After reading 'The Twelve Tasks of Heracles', explore its many funny and serious aspects.
- Ask the children to divide a sheet of paper into four: 'Layout', 'Tasks', 'Characters' and 'Words'.
- Investigate page three of the myth. Ask: *What do you notice? Are the cartoons full and busy? Does the page look funny or serious? Why?* Emphasise that choosing 'funny' or 'serious' is a personal reaction; either is correct. After paired discussion, ask for written answers under 'Layout'. Encourage a sentence or two and reference to details in the style and presentation of page three.
- Now ask the children to scan pages two to four, where Heracles performs his tasks. Do they find most of these scenes serious or funny? They record their reactions and reasons under 'Tasks'.
- Repeat the exercise for 'Characters' (for the whole story), asking: *Are characters presented humorously? Does someone make you laugh?* Remind them to refer directly to the myth.
- In the last section, 'Words', the children should study all the written text, particularly the speech bubbles. Is the language amusing?
- Finally, ask the children to analyse their results. Do they find this myth mainly serious or mainly funny? Ask them to write a sentence explaining their conclusion.

> **Differentiation**
> **For older/more confident learners:** Consider additional aspects, such as figures' positions and facial expressions.
> **For younger/less confident learners:** Encourage partner discussion, written reactions and oral reasons.

Plot, character and setting

Exploring language

Objective: To explore how different texts appeal to readers using varied sentence structures and descriptive language.
What you need: Copies of *Greek Myths*, writing materials.

What to do
● After reading 'Daedalus and Icarus', discuss that variety in writing keeps readers interested.
● Investigate sentence structure in this story. Can the children identify a simple sentence on page one? (*Daedalus was a brilliant craftsman; Talos was a clever boy; He invented the… potter's wheel.*) Revise complex sentences – they have a main clause with one or more subordinate clauses; a conjunction connects the clauses – and identify examples. (*So, with his son Icarus,… welcomed him. The goddess… flew away.*) Ask the children to write, under the heading 'Sentence structure', one or two sentences about how sentences are used in the myth.

● Suggest that there is also variety in the punctuation within the sentences. Let pairs scan the punctuation, then ask: *What could replace the dash and colons on page two?* (Full stops.) *Has the author made better choices?* (Hers maintain flow and suggest excitement.) Under the heading 'Punctuation', ask the children to write about its effect on their reading.
● Consider the flow of the writing. Notice the last strip on page one, where one sentence covers two captions. Invite pairs to investigate pages two and three. Ask: *Do sentences continue across captions? Is suspense built up?* Under the heading 'Connections', let the children write a sentence about the effect of this technique.

Differentiation
For older/more confident learners: Ask children to consider the writer's descriptions too.
For younger/less confident learners: Limit children's writing to phrases or single sentences.

Moving on

Objective: To identify and make notes of the main points of sections of text.
What you need: Copies of *Greek Myths*, photocopiable page 17, writing materials.
Cross-curricular link: Geography.

What to do
● After reading 'Perseus and the Gorgon's Head', comment on its length of time and the number of places visited.
● Guide the children in scanning page one, suggesting that the last strip here is the start of the main story. Give out photocopiable page 17 and let the children add to the first box, drawing Perseus and writing an explanation of why he is leaving.
● Now work together again, scanning page two. Ask: *Where does Perseus travel? What happens? How is time emphasised?* (Four small pictures within one frame; scenery changes; time references, such as, *for many days, The next day, That night.*)

● Suggest that Hermes' visit marks the halfway point of the journey. Locate it on the photocopiable sheet, for the children to add a sentence about the help Hermes gives.
● Direct the children to *after a year away* in the second strip on the last page. Match this to the final box on the photocopiable sheet.
● Ask the children to use the photocopiable sheet's headings to complete the other boxes. Let partners help each other to check places and events on the journey, and the devices and words expressing the passing of time.

Differentiation
For older/more confident learners: Ask the children for more detailed writing.
For younger/less confident learners: Suggest mainly pictorial recording with place and character labels. Expect one time reference for each half of the story.

Plot, character and setting

Choosing heroes

> **Objective:** To explore how and why authors write.
> **What you need:** Copies of *Greek Myths*, writing materials.
> **Cross-curricular link:** PSHE.

What to do
- Do this activity after reading the myths about Perseus and Theseus.
- Refer to *retold* on the book's cover. Comment that in rewriting the original myths, Marcia Williams emphasises details and adapts characters as she prefers.
- Point out *heroic* in the last caption of 'Theseus and the Minotaur'. Ask pairs to tell each other what they now expect of a hero in these myths. Share ideas and list these characteristics on the board, for example selfless care for others, courage, defeating a monster, having magical help, but doing something foolish.
- Ask the children to divide their paper in two, labelling one half 'Perseus' and the other 'Theseus'. Guide partners in scanning the two myths for evidence of the first point from the list on the board. Direct them to where Perseus tells his mother not to worry and sets off on a deadly mission. Ask: *How does Theseus show similar selflessness?* (He goes to Crete with the victims.) Ask the children to write about these points on their paper.
- Invite pairs to search for evidence of the other characteristics listed. For each, they should write a sentence to summarise it.
- Finally, hold a discussion to decide which of the two men Marcia Williams might choose as the book's hero.

> **Differentiation**
> **For older/more confident learners:** Add two more characteristics: being popular; physical strength.
> **For younger/less confident learners:** Reduce writing to notes and phrases, and omit one characteristic.

Who's got the power?

> **Objective:** To interrogate texts to deepen and clarify understanding and response.
> **What you need:** Copies of *Greek Myths*, photocopiable page 18, writing materials.
> **Cross-curricular link:** PSHE.

What to do
- After finishing the book, suggest that the relative powers of gods and humans is an important theme.
- Ask pairs to tell each other, without checking in the book, where the gods live and how humans came into being.
- Study the opening strips of 'Pandora's Box'. Identify *In the beginning; Mount Olympus; made people out of clay* and *breathed life into them.* Let the pairs check each other's information.
- Point out that when humans try to behave disrespectfully, the gods punish them as a reminder of their greater power and eminent position.
- Direct the children to Prometheus' trick 'sacrifice' to Zeus. Ask: *What is the punishment?* (Zeus puts out all fire on earth.) Let the children complete the first section of photocopiable page 18, which is all about power.
- Invite the children to work in pairs to complete the remaining sections. They need to identify the myth, scan the text and pictures; and discuss the human's (or giant's) action, the god's reaction and the punishment.
- Bring the class together to discuss answers. Do the children think the gods use their power fairly?

> **Differentiation**
> **For older/more confident learners:** Add this section to the sheet: 'Pandora opens the box'.
> **For younger/less confident learners:** Allow pictorial recording and limited writing. Direct the children to places in the myths.

Understanding character

- Draw lines to join the two most suitable adjectives to each cartoon.
- Then write your own adjectives for Pandora's behaviour. Draw a line from each of those, too.

argumentative   bad-tempered   clever   inquisitive   sulky

sly   curious   nosy   greedy

Pandora gets what Pandora wants.

I'll just sit here and wait, then!

Open that box at once, you old miser! I know it is full of jewels.

I want clothes!

stubborn   determined   cunning   angry

demanding   nagging   self-centred   brave

- Your own adjectives for Pandora.

Plot, character and setting

SECTION
4

Collecting information

- Fill in what you know and what you still have to learn about this story.
- Then draw and write what you think might happen next.

What I know about…	What I don't yet know about…
Periander	
Arion	
The sailors	

What I think will happen…

Moving on

- Draw and write about important places and events on Perseus' journey.
- Quote words that show the passing of time.

Setting off	On the journey	Proof of time	Stopping
Perseus leaves his mother.			Perseus is visited by Hermes.

Setting off	On the journey	Proof of time	Setting off
Perseus leaves Hermes.			Perseus arrives at Seriphos.

READ & RESPOND: Activities based on Greek Myths

Who's got the power?

- Think about these events where people show their power.
- Draw and write about which gods become angry and the punishments they give.

	Which god becomes angry and why?	What punishment is given?
Prometheus snaps off a piece of the sun.		
Young Heracles gets stronger and stronger and stronger.		
Daedalus pushes Talos off a roof.		
Arachne shows her brilliance at weaving.		

SCHOLASTIC
www.scholastic.co.uk

READ & RESPOND: Activities based on Greek Myths

Talk about it

Stop the story

> **Objective:** To comment constructively on plays and performances, discussing effects and how they are achieved.
> **What you need:** Copies of *Greek Myths*, photocopiable page 22.
> **Cross-curricular link:** Drama.

What to do
- Use this activity after reading 'Pandora's Box'.
- Explain or revise the term 'freeze-frame': children take on the roles of story figures and create a still picture of a particular moment in the story.
- Create groups of four and give each group a card from photocopiable page 22. Ask them to work out a freeze-frame for that story moment, without looking at the book.
- Allow about five minutes for discussion and rehearsal. Encourage every member of the group to contribute to the decision-making.
- Ask each group to present their freeze-frame, looked at by the rest of the class. Can the audience identify the story moment? Do they recognise the characters? Select characters to step out of the tableau and tell the class what they are thinking. Alternatively, ask the class to suggest what a character seems to be thinking.
- Comment on the importance of facial expression and body language in freeze-frames. Discuss in groups, then as a class, which expressions and body language the children found particularly revealing.
- Finish with groups repeating their freeze-frames in story order, this time with more expressive faces and bold body language.

> **Differentiation**
> **For older/more confident learners:** Let the children create a freeze-frame for a story moment of their choice.
> **For younger/less confident learners:** Move among groups, offering support and suggestions.

Persuasive talk

> **Objective:** To sustain conversation, explain or give reasons for their views or choices.
> **What you need:** Copies of *Greek Myths*.
> **Cross-curricular link:** PSHE.

What to do
- Read 'The Twelve Tasks of Heracles'. Discuss how long the tasks take: Heracles complains of being *fed up* after ten tasks in ten years.
- Remind the children that some of the creatures have to be captured alive. Identify Cerberus, the golden-horned deer, the savage boar and the fire-breathing bull.
- Set up a scenario in which Heracles meets these talking animals and persuades them to come with him. Organise the children into pairs, one taking the role of Heracles, the other the deer. On your signal, let pairs begin their dialogue (made up as they go along). Keep this improvisation short.
- Signal the children to stop. Choose one or two pairs to remain in character while other children question them about how they feel. Does Heracles feel he has done enough to persuade the deer? Is the deer willing to go or reluctant?
- Now ask the pairs to hold a conversation between Heracles and the boar, with partners exchanging the role of Heracles. Choose a different pair to be questioned by the class. Repeat the exercise for Cerberus and the bull.
- Afterwards, ask pairs to decide which animal seems most willing to go with Heracles. Share conclusions as a class.

> **Differentiation**
> **For older/more confident learners:** Ask pairs to persuade other animals to come and frighten the King: Diomedes' horses, and Geryon's cattle and two-headed dog.
> **For younger/less confident learners:** Provide conversation openers to inspire ideas.

Talk about it

Listen to your conscience

Objective: To use some drama strategies to explore stories or issues.
What you need: Copies of *Greek Myths*.
Cross-curricular links: Drama, PSHE.

What to do

- Use this activity after reading 'Orpheus and Eurydice', 'Daedalus and Icarus' and 'Theseus and the Minotaur'.
- Point out that in many of the myths, the hero faces an important decision. Refer to the beginning of 'Daedalus and Icarus', when Daedalus is on the roof of the temple.
- Divide the class into two groups: Group A represents Daedalus' good side, and Group B his bad side. One side opposes the other in his mind, as he struggles with jealousy. Ask Group A to think of short comments to say to stop Daedalus pushing Talos. Ask Group B to think of remarks to encourage him.
- Arrange the two groups into parallel lines facing each other. Take the role of Daedalus and walk down the 'conscience alley' between the lines, nodding to children to prompt them to speak their lines. At the end of the alley, having listened to your conscience (their voices), make your decision.
- Let children take turns playing Daedalus and repeat the exercise. Does every Daedalus reach the same decision?
- Use other situations, for example: *Should Theseus leave Ariadne on the island? Should Orpheus check that Eurydice is following?*
- Create shorter conscience alleys so more children can listen to their conscience.

Differentiation
For older/more confident learners: Ask the children to plan a conscience-alley situation for Pandora.
For younger/less confident learners: Provide sample comments and let the children speak with a partner.

Quite a story!

Objective: To tell stories effectively and convey detailed information coherently for listeners.
What you need: Copies of *Greek Myths*, photocopiable page 23, writing materials.
Cross-curricular link: Geography.

What to do

- After reading 'Theseus and the Minotaur', set the scene. Rumours have spread in Athens about the amazing return of Theseus and the youths and maidens. People want to hear what happened. Theseus, the youths and maidens are attending a palace reception so they can tell their story.
- Establish the important events in the story: the stormy journey; the first night in Crete; help from Ariadne; being thrown into the Labyrinth; Theseus killing the Minotaur; being let out by Ariadne; the journey home.
- Help the children to decide which character to play: Theseus, a youth or a maiden. Explain that, as storytellers, they must organise their facts, describe their feelings and include details (perhaps with information or memories known only to them).
- Give out photocopiable page 23 for the children to make notes and sketches to recall what happened. Emphasise that they will be *telling*, not reading their stories, so they will use these cue cards only as prompts.
- When they feel ready, let the children practise their storytelling on partners. Then organise storytelling groups, so everyone experiences speaking to a group.

Differentiation
For older/more confident learners: Ask the children to tell their story as King Minos.
For younger/less confident learners: Reduce the number of cards and suggest the children make pictorial and one-word prompts.

Talk about it

Changing the dialogue

Objective: To develop scripts based on improvisation.
What you need: Copies of *Greek Myths*, photocopiable page 24, writing materials.
Cross-curricular link: PSHE.

What to do

● After finishing the book, ask: *Is dialogue important in the myths? Why?* (It influences mood, plot and characterisation.)
● Direct the children to the captions and speech bubbles when Arion, on board ship with the sailors, is returning home. Re-read the dialogue – the children reading as the sailors, you as Arion. Suggest that if the writer, when editing her story, had decided to be kinder to the sailors and save them from punishment, she could have changed the dialogue.
● Put the children into pairs: one as Arion, one as a sailor. Ask them to improvise new dialogue

so that the sailor will not be banished later. Afterwards ask: *Have you improved the sailor's character? How much have you changed the story?*
● Repeat the exercise with the conversation between Arachne and the disguised Athene. Encourage pairs to think about the effect they want from their new dialogue: more humour, altered characters or changed plot? Let the class listen to and comment on some conversations.
● Give out individual copies of photocopiable page 24. Advise the children to decide the effect they want to achieve before they write.

Differentiation
For older/more confident learners: Ask the children to develop one of the conversations into a playscript for that scene.
For younger/less confident learners: Let partners continue to work together, rehearsing words before they write.

In the hot-seat

Objective: To infer characters' feelings in fiction and consequences in logical explanations.
What you need: Copies of *Greek Myths*, writing materials, costume props (optional).
Cross-curricular link: Drama.

What to do

● After finishing the book, suggest that readers may want more detail about the gods' and goddesses' reasons for doing things. For example: *Why does Zeus send thunderbolts? Why is Hera so hateful to Heracles? Does Athene make Icarus fall?*
● Focus on Zeus. Ask the children, in pairs, to discuss, agree on and write two questions they want to ask him. Combine the pairs into groups of four to compare questions. Then ask each group to decide on just two group questions to ask.
● Revise the term 'hot-seat': a role play in which a character is questioned by readers or audience.

Put yourself in the hot-seat as Zeus. Turn away and make a change to your appearance, for example add a sash or crown of leaves. Turn back to the children as Zeus; your speech and answers must be in role.
● After putting their two questions and making notes on your answers, let the groups discuss what Zeus revealed about his personality and motivation. Compare findings as a class.
● Select a different god or goddess: Athene, Hera or Hermes. Repeat the exercise as a group activity, with one group member taking the hot-seat to answer the others' questions.

Differentiation
For older/more confident learners: Ask the children to make close references to the text both in questions and answers.
For younger/less confident learners: Prompt the children on points to ask about.

Talk about it

Stop the story

● Create freeze-frames of these moments from 'Pandora's Box'.

1. Zeus, Athene and Hera are on Mount Olympus. Prometheus has made a human out of clay. Zeus is breathing life into the clay person.	2. On Olympus, Hera and Zeus look inside the trick sacrifice sack. Hera is disgusted; Zeus is furious. On earth, Prometheus laughs and a man smiles.
3. From Olympus, Zeus sprinkles water on earth to put out fire. Hera, watching, claps her hands with delight. On earth, people huddle together, shivering.	4. Prometheus reaches up and breaks off a piece of sun. Some people on earth, watch, pleased. An angry Zeus watches from Olympus.
5. Prometheus lies chained to a rock. A vulture is tearing at his liver. Zeus and Hera, pleased, watch from Mount Olympus.	6. Epimetheus sleeps in a chair. Pandora holds the box and is about to open it. She is very excited. Zeus and Athene, disappointed, watch from Olympus, shaking their heads.

Talk about it

Quite a story!

● Complete these cards. Use them to tell the story as someone who went into the Labyrinth.

Introducing yourself Who you are? What was your journey to Crete like?	**The night in Crete** Did you sleep? Did anything wake you up?
Inside the Labyrinth Were you terrified? Did you stay near the entrance?	**The Minotaur** Did you see or hear the Minotaur? How did you know it was dead?
Leaving at night How did you escape from the Labyrinth? Did you have help?	**Back home** How do you feel now?

Talk about it

Changing the dialogue

- Write new dialogue for these situations.
- What effect do your changes have on the story?

1. Arion is returning home with his prizes

Sailor: You have won so much gold!

Arion: _____

Sailor: _____

Arion: _____

Sailor: _____

Arion: _____

My changes have this effect: _____

_____

_____

2. Athene visits Arachne in disguise

Arachne: How can I help you, good woman?

Athene: _____

Arachne: _____

Athene: _____

Arachne: _____

Athene: _____

My changes have this effect: _____

_____

_____

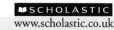

Get writing

Today's Pandora

> **Objective:** To use layout, format, graphics and illustrations for different purposes.
> **What you need:** Copies of *Greek Myths*, photocopiable page 28, writing materials.
> **Cross-curricular link:** Art and design.

What to do

● After reading 'Pandora's Box', suggest that the myth has two stories: Prometheus' and Pandora's. Explain that the children are going to write a modern version of Pandora's story.

● Identify four main parts: *Opening* (introduces setting and characters); *Events* (Pandora learns about the box); *Climax* (Pandora opens the box); *Ending* (the aftermath).

● Invite pairs, and then the whole class, to share ideas for a modern version. Ask: *Where is it set?* (A classroom) *Who is the main character?* (Dora.) *What happens?* (Dora sees a '*Do not touch!*' sign on the printer.) *What is the climax?* (Dora presses

'Print'.) *How does it end?* (The whole school computer network crashes.)

● Demonstrate note-writing on an enlarged copy of photocopiable page 28. Use a different simple story; perhaps an updated 'Little Red Riding Hood'. Alongside words and phrases, use quick, annotated sketches to plan cartoon frames.

● Give out individual copies of photocopiable 28. In pairs, let the children discuss their story ideas, then make notes.

● Use further writing sessions for the children to write and draw their modern cartoon stories.

> **Differentiation**
> **For older/more confident learners:** Ask the children to include one or two time connectives or dialogue words in each section.
> **For younger/less confident learners:** Let the children work in pairs, writing only one or two notes for each section.

Detailed writing

> **Objective:** To show imagination through the language used to create emphasis, humour, atmosphere or suspense.
> **What you need:** Copies of *Greek Myths*, writing materials.

What to do

● After reading 'The Twelve Tasks of Heracles', comment that this 'busy' myth has more action than the other myths squeezed into the same number of pages. Ask: *Which does more storytelling here: words or pictures?* (Pictures, because they are more numerous and more detailed.)

● Identify double rows of cartoons within single frames, with single captions. Ask: *Could Marcia Williams have removed some cartoons and replaced them with text?* A narrow strip of cartoons would remain, but two or three sentences would lengthen the caption. *What changes would this need?* (Descriptive detail, atmospheric language, information about mood and feelings.)

● Examine the first task's caption and pictures. Ask the children to consider the place, the lion, and the feelings of Heracles and the King. What words would they use to describe them? Share these before asking the children to write the heading 'Task one' on their paper and then add two sentences to the caption.

● Examine the seventh task's cartoons and caption. Think about the place, suspense and Heracles' efforts and feelings. Under 'Task seven', the children write their additions to the caption.

● Repeat this for the twelfth task. Ask pairs: *What is the journey like? What is the atmosphere? What is Heracles' mood? Why?*

> **Differentiation**
> **For older/more confident learners:** Expect more writing and greater emphasis on atmosphere and mood.
> **For younger/less confident learners:** Accept one sentence for each task.

Get writing

Choose your ending

Objective: To make decisions about form and purpose, identify success criteria and use them to evaluate their writing.
What you need: Copies of *Greek Myths*, writing materials.
Cross-curricular link: Citizenship.

What to do
● Re-read the final two pages of 'Daedalus and Icarus', from the point where Icarus loses his first feather. Invite the children in pairs to explain the job of a story ending. Compare ideas, agreeing on essentials: loose ends are tied up, plot questions are answered, plot problems are resolved.
● Identify some of these features in 'Daedalus and Icarus'. The myth has returned to the opening frames' relationship between Daedalus and Talos; the problem of Daedalus' guilt has been addressed; the question of whether the gods will punish Daedalus has been answered.

● Ask the children whether any questions have not been answered. (For example, *Will Daedalus continue to feel guilt and fear? Will the gods return Icarus in a different form? Is Daedalus marooned on this island?*)
● Invite the children to think of alternative endings. Let them exchange ideas in pairs before sharing some as a class.
● Now re-read the myth's first two pages, and say that Marcia Williams has stopped here! Ask the children to finish the story for her. Suggest that they make brief planning notes before writing their new ending for the myth.

Differentiation
For older/more confident learners: Ask the children to write a second alternative ending.
For younger/less confident learners: Suggest that the children sketch their ending before they start writing the text.

Gods, goddesses and heroes

Objective: To summarise and shape material and ideas from different sources to write convincing and informative non-narrative texts.
What you need: Copies of *Greek Myths*, writing materials, internet access.
Cross-curricular link: ICT.

What to do
● After finishing the book, ask the children to divide their paper into four sections: Zeus, Hera, Athene and Hermes.
● What do they learn about Zeus as they scan 'Pandora's Box'? Make simple notes.
● Investigate Hera: her ill-temper and position as Zeus' wife in 'Pandora's Box'; her spite and determination in 'The Twelve Tasks of Heracles'. Remind the children to write in note form.
● Take one myth at a time. In the same way, identify Athene's kindness in 'Perseus and the Gorgon's Head' and 'Daedalus and Icarus', and her punishment of wrongdoing.

● What do readers learn about Hermes? (*Messenger-god; fond of Perseus.*)
● In the last myth, contrast Zeus' quick temper with Athene's patience in giving Arachne a chance. Ask: *What does the owl symbolise?* (Wisdom.) *What skill does Athene have?* (Weaving.)
● For additional notes, look at a website such as the BBC.
● Ask the children to develop their notes into information text or a website about the gods. Support the children with their use of layout, headings, paragraphs, pictures and hyperlinks.

Differentiation
For older/more confident learners: Ask the children to research and write about Poseidon and Apollo.
For younger/less confident learners: Let the children work in pairs and write about two or three gods.

Get writing

The dogs' tales

> **Objective:** To choose and combine words and images and other features for particular effects.
> **What you need:** Copies of *Greek Myths*, photocopiable page 29, writing materials.
> **Cross-curricular link:** History.

What to do
● After finishing the book, find the dog in the final strip of 'Theseus and the Minotaur'. Ask: *Where else is it in the myth?* (The frames showing Theseus' departure.)
● Comment that other myths also feature ordinary dogs. Locate them in 'Arion and the Dolphins', 'Orpheus and Eurydice', and 'Perseus and the Gorgon's Head'. Read the accompanying captions: the dogs are not mentioned. Suggest that these dogs perhaps seem like modern observers of ancient happenings.
● Direct the children to the third strip on the first page of 'Daedalus and Icarus': one frame has a speech bubble, the other has thought bubbles. How are they distinguished?
● Give out photocopiable page 29. Ask pairs to locate the first myth, the relevant part of the story and the dog without a bubble. Let the pairs compare ideas for a bubble. Will words be thought or spoken? Will they add humour? Suggest that partners try out words on each other before writing them.
● Let the children work through the other cartoons in this way, writing a speech or thought bubble for each dog. Afterwards, invite the class to view and listen to each other's work.

> **Differentiation**
> **For older/more confident learners:** Ask for bubbles for the dogs in 'The Twelve Tasks of Heracles' and 'Arachne versus Athene'.
> **For younger/less confident learners:** Provide vocabulary or sentence starters.

Book review

> **Objective:** To share and compare reasons for reading preferences, extending the range of books read.
> **What you need:** Copies of *Greek Myths*, photocopiable page 30, writing materials, published book reviews.
> **Cross-curricular link:** PSHE.

What to do
● Ask the children to tell each other, in pairs, what a book review is. Share ideas and show the children some examples. Explain that there is no set format, but investigate common features: the book's title, author and, if appropriate, illustrator; information about or a synopsis of the book (without giving away too much); personal likes or dislikes; opinion about its suitability for other readers.
● Hold a class discussion to share opinions on *Greek Myths*. Emphasise to the children that their opinions are not right or wrong – tastes are personal – but their views should be supported with reference to the book. Ask, for example: *What did the cover lead you to expect? Were you surprised by the cartoon format? Which myth did you particularly enjoy? What did you find the most and least successful aspects of the book's style?*
● Give out photocopiable page 30 for the children to write their review of *Greek Myths*. Remind them to write whole sentences for most sections.

> **Differentiation**
> **For older/more confident learners:** Suggest to the children that they use their completed sheet to help them write a polished review, suitable for a magazine or website.
> **For younger/less confident learners:** Provide suggestions and encourage partner discussion when selecting and explaining what is most liked or disliked.

Get writing

Today's Pandora

- Create a modern version of Pandora's Box below.

Opening

Setting _____

_____

Main character _____

_____

_____

_____

The main event

The forbidden thing _____

_____

Who looks after it? _____

_____

_____

_____

Climax

What does she do? _____

_____

What happens then? Is there a
disaster? _____

_____

_____

_____

Ending

How she feels afterwards

_____

Is there a happy ending?

_____

_____

_____

Get writing

The dogs' tales

● These animals look like modern dogs taking an interest in ancient events. Write a speech or thought bubble for each dog.

Periander settled back to enjoy some of Arion's finest singing.

Orpheus was inconsolable and would neither eat nor drink.

King Acrisius of Argos was a worried man. When Danae bore a baby boy…

Theseus prepared to sail for Crete.

Get writing

Book review

● Write your review of *Greek Myths*.

Author _____

Illustrator _____

About the book _____

_____

_____

_____

My favourite part _____

_____

_____

_____

My least favourite part _____

_____

_____

_____

Who would enjoy this book? _____

_____

_____

_____

My rating for this book.

☆ ☆ ☆ ☆ ☆

Assessment

Assessment advice

Power is central to this book. It is present in: heroes who overcome monsters; the strength of sun, thunder and sea; magical objects; and, in particular, the gods' control over mankind. Exploring the theme of power is an effective way to assess the children's grasp of the myths and their plots and characters.

Use drama improvisation to investigate the power struggle between Zeus and Prometheus in 'Pandora's Box'. Focus on the scenes where Prometheus sends a trick sacrifice and then breaks off some sun. Observe the children's body language and facial expression as they show Zeus' feelings. Through improvised dialogue in pairs, assess the children's recognition of Zeus' rage and thoughts of punishment, and Prometheus' regret and acknowledgement of Zeus' greater power.

Still in their pairs, ask the children to take turns as Zeus in the hot-seat, explaining when, how and why he uses his power against mankind. Assess the children's understanding of Zeus' motives: expecting respect from people, and revenge when he doesn't get it.

Revenge is another theme that runs through the book. If promises are broken or hurt inflicted, gods and people always exact revenge. To assess the children's understanding, revise the plot of 'Arion and the Dolphins'. Ask children to act out a dialogue between Periander and Arion when Arion returns home alone. With the children in role as Periander, ask: *What do you think about the sailors? What will you do?* Watch for body and facial language, as well as words, expressing vengeful thoughts. Then question the children in role as Arion when Periander wants the sailors killed. Do they recognise Arion's gentler nature and Periander's gradual relenting? Do they understand that some revenge or punishment is essential?

What do they think?

> **Assessment focus:** To deduce, infer or interpret information, events or ideas from texts.
> **What you need:** Copies of *Greek Myths*, photocopiable page 32, writing materials.

What to do

● Refer first to the final strips of 'Theseus and the Minotaur'. Can the children explain to their partners why Theseus does not change the sail to white? (Forgetfulness, likely caused by the gods' revenge for his leaving Ariadne.) Point out that Marcia Williams does not state that the gods are responsible, so, what makes us think that the gods are involved? (Similar events in other myths imply it.)

● Hand out photocopiable page 32. Ask the children to find each situation in the text. Suggest to the children that they pretend to be the characters and write what is in their minds. (Less confident writers could provide oral answers.) The activity will allow you to check the children's understanding of the myths and then assess their ability to deduce implied information.

● Expect the children to give these sorts of answers:

● Epimetheus worries that Zeus will know if he disobeys Prometheus, and will be vengeful.

● Pandora imagines that there are jewels in the box; she wants to have them.

● Eurydice fears that Orpheus will turn round and the gods will separate them.

● Orpheus suspects that the King and Queen are tricking him and Eurydice is not following him.

● Arachne believes that she is being clever and is right to boast.

● Her father fears that Arachne will be punished by Athene.

Assessment

What do they think?

● Sometimes, a reader can work out what is in a character's mind. What are these characters thinking at these times?

Epimetheus worries…

Pandora imagines…

1. Epimeheus and Pandora struggle over the locked box.

Eurydice fears…

Orpheus suspects…

2. Eurydice follows Orpheus through the underworld.

Her father fears…

Arachne believes…

3. Arachne tells her father that she is a better weaver than Athene.